CONT

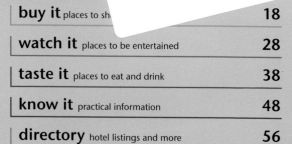

Map references are denoted in the text by ❶ Downtown Manhattan
❷ Central Manhattan ❸ Subway ❹ Midtown ❺ Theater District *(p.36)*

new york places to see

Known as 'the city that never sleeps' because there is always *something* going on, New York welcomes over 50 million tourists every year. Though there are five boroughs — Manhattan, Brooklyn, Queens, the Bronx and Staten Island — that are all connected by myriad bridges, subways, trains and ferries, it is Manhattan's many attractions, from world-class shopping to celebrated restaurants and superb museums, that draw the crowds. Winters here are blustery, summers can be hot, spring and autumn are temperate, but the Big Apple offers attractions to suit all interests and seasons.

see it places to see

Sights

American Museum of Natural History ❷ 2L

With 32 million exhibits, this shrine to natural history is the largest of its kind in the world. Must-see attractions include the world-renowned Dinosaur Halls and the awe-inspiring Rose Center for Earth and Space, a mammoth glass cube enclosing the most technologically advanced space theater in existence; witness the Big Bang or take a cosmic voyage through 13 billion

New York Views

Get the classic view of the Manhattan skyline and the Statue of Liberty for free from the romantic Staten Island Ferry, New York's sightseeing bargain (boats leave round the clock every 30 mins). For the best views over the city, head for the 86th floor of the Empire State Building (see p.7).

The lights of Broadway

light-years from the Milky Way to the 'edge' of the universe. *Adm. Open 10am–5.45pm daily. T: 212 769 5100, www.amnh.org*

Broadway & Times Square ❶ 2H/❷ 2I/❹/❺

From dramas to musical extravaganzas, Broadway (see p.34) is the place to catch a show. At the heart of it all is Times Square, the "crossroads of the world" and home to MTV, Condé Nast, the 52-story steel-and-glass New York Times tower, the giant Nasdaq video screen and the interactive Madame Tussaud's Wax Museum (*234 W 42nd St btw Seventh & Eighth Aves,*

Times Square

www.nycwax.com). The Times Square Alliance offers official Times Square Walking Tours, leaving from the Times Square Visitors Center (*see p.50*). Three tours daily (*$25pp*), *1560 Broadway btw 46th & 47th Sts, T: 212 452 5283, www.timessquarenyc.org*

Brooklyn Bridge ❶ 5B

Completed in 1883 after 14 years, the Brooklyn Bridge is an engineering marvel once described by Lewis Mumford as 'the most completely satisfying structure of any kind.' Come at sunset for classic views of Manhattan from the pedestrian walkway that traverses the length of the bridge, or, for cinematic views of the bridge, go to the end of Pier 17 at the South Street Seaport (see p.13).

Bryant Park ❶ 3H

Located behind the main branch of the NY Public Library (see p.12), the

Skating in Bryant Park

park has free wireless access, alfresco cafés and food kiosks and restroom facilities. This outdoor haven draws natives and visitors with its classic French garden design. In summertime enjoy free concerts and films and a charming carousel, while in the winter there is free ice-skating.
Sixth Ave btw 40th & 42nd Sts, T: 212 768 4242, www.bryantpark.org

Central Park ❷ 3J-3O

Twice the size of Monaco, New York's lovely green carpet is an oasis of peace in the heart of the urban jungle. Hire a rowboat, bike or gondola at the Loeb Boathouse, go ice-skating at the open-air Wollman Rink in the winter, enjoy free concerts on the Great Lawn, or see Shakespeare in the Park at the Delacorte Theater (see box, p.31). Just off Fifth Avenue, you can step into a steamy rainforest or an icy snowscape at the Central Park Zoo with a nearby Children's Zoo where the kids can greet the animals.
Central Park Zoo and Tisch Children's Zoo: Fifth Ave at E 64th St, T: 212 439 6500, www.centralparkzoo.com

New York for Free

MoMA (see p.11) is free on Fridays from 4pm-8pm. The 9/11 Memorial and Museum, ❶ 3B (see p.15), has free admission. Check *www.clubfreetime.com* for a monthly listing of free or low-cost museums, concerts, walks and special events.

Central Park boating lake

Chinatown ❶ 4B-4C

With 150,000 to 250,000 people crammed into two square miles, this is the largest Chinatown in the US.

It's chaotic and exciting, bursting with colorful restaurants (see p.40), herb shops and fruit and fish markets. Shop along Canal and Mott Streets for everything from woks and mah-jong sets to gold jewelry.

Chrysler Building ❶ 4H

Opened in 1930, this 77-story art deco tribute to Walter P. Chrysler was briefly the tallest skyscraper in the world. It soon lost its title to the Empire State, but its glittering crown

The 77-story art deco Chrysler Building

has ensured that it remains one of the city's best-loved landmarks. Its construction shrouded in secrecy, the spire was built in a fire shaft that was raised to reveal a stainless-steel extravaganza covered in automotive motifs and gargoyles modeled on Chrysler hood ornaments. The elaborate lobby is a monument to art deco and was once a Chrysler car showroom. *Open office hours, lobby only. 405 Lexington Ave at 42nd St.*

The Cloisters off map

A satellite location of the Metropolitan Museum of Art (see p.11), the Cloisters has a stunning collection of more than 5,000 medieval artifacts housed in a complex of reassembled European abbeys in a dramatic position overlooking the Hudson River. Star exhibits include the exquisitely delicate 16th-century "Unicorn Tapestries," salvaged from a chateau at Verteuil, France, where they were used for keeping frost off vegetables. *Adm. Open 9.30am- 5.35pm Tue-Thu, 9.30am-9pm Sun, Fri & Sat. Fort Tryon Park, Washington Heights, T: 212 923 3700, www.metmuseum.org*

Cooper-Hewitt National Design Museum ❷ 3M

Treasure trove of 250,000 articles of historical and contemporary design,

---

AKA NY

In 1968 the Artists' Association named the colony south of Houston Street 'SoHo', ❶ 3C-3D. After SoHo came TriBeCa, ❶ 3C, the Triangle below Canal Street; then NoLiTa, ❶ 4D, North of Little Italy. Brooklyn's Dumbo, ❶ 6B, Down Under the Manhattan Bridge Overpass, is home to artists and musicians, while the Meatpacking District, ❶ 2E – is just too cool for acronyms.

from swords and cutlery to furniture by Frank Lloyd Wright, in the former home of philanthropist Andrew Carnegie. The Museum has recently undergone major renovations making exhibitions truly interactive via 4K resolution touchscreen tables. *Adm. 91st St at Fifth Ave, T: 212 849 8400, www.cooperhewitt.org*

Empire State Building ❶ 3G

Elevators whisk you up to an observation deck on the 86th floor for incredible 360° views of the city. The deck is at its romantic best at night, with the city glittering into the horizon, or in a thunderstorm, when static build-up is so intense that the lips of kissing couples discharge sparks. Lines are long; pre-purchasing tickets saves time. *Adm. Open 8am-2am daily (last elevators 1.15am). 350 Fifth Ave btw 33rd & 34th Sts, T: 212 736 3100, www.esbnyc.com*

Frick Collection ❷ 3K

Art collections don't get better than this; the electrifying collection of Old Masters, including Rembrandt, Turner, Holbein and Vermeer, was assembled in the 19th century by the steel magnate, Henry Clay Frick. This was his elegant home, which was first opened to the public in 1935. It also has collections of Oriental rugs and French furniture. *Adm. Open 10am-6pm Tue-Sat, 11am-5pm Sun, 10 E 70th St at Fifth Ave, T: 212 288 0700, www.frick.org*

In reflection: the Empire State Building

Grand Central Terminal ❶ 4H

Watching Manhattan's commuters zigzagging across the magnificent 375-ft x 125-ft (114 x 38-m) marble concourse is one of New York's most mesmerizing sights. Look up to view the incredible Sky Ceiling, showcasing the twinkling constellations of the city's winter sky. Drink cocktails on the west balcony at the ultra chic Campbell Apartment (*T: 212 953 0409*), located in the paneled offices of the 1920s tycoon John Campbell. *Multilingual Audio & downloadable tours (adm) and information on self-guided tours are available from the information booth. T: 212 340 2345, www.grandcentralterminal.com*

Grand Central Station's clock is perhaps its most recognizable feature

Greenwich Village ❶ 3E

Once upon a time Greenwich Village was home to many of America's bohemians and artists: the Beats, Jack Kerouac and Bob Dylan, to name but a few. Unfortunately, high real estate prices have driven much of the Village's creative community to the outer boroughs, but the neighborhood is still one of the loveliest in the city. Some of the world's best jazz clubs are situated here, along with some superb restaurants, charming cafés and boutiques.

Guggenheim Museum ❷ 3M

Upstaging almost everything else on Fifth Avenue, Frank Lloyd Wright's maverick spiral is home to a stellar 20th-century collection by Kandinsky, Chagall, Cézanne, Picasso, Degas and Van Gogh and Van Gogh. There's also a café, a stylish restaurant, The Wright, and a museum boutique. *Adm. Open 10am-5.45pm Sun-Wed & Fri, 10am-7.45pm Sat; closed Thu. 1071 Fifth Ave at 89th St, T: 212 423 3500, www.guggenheim.org*

The High Line in Chelsea

integrative landscapes and public art installations, not to mention sweeping Hudson River vistas.
Open 7am-11pm daily. Gansevoort St to W 34th St, btw 10th & 11th Aves, T: 212 206 9922, www.thehighline.org

Hudson River Park ❶ 3C-1H

An enormous ongoing project for revamping the waterfront, this park stretching for five miles (81 km) from Battery Park to 59th Street has developed the Hudson River piers and waterfront with a spectacular green-and-blue oasis of boathouses, blade- and bikeways, sportsfields, sundecks, playgrounds, lawns and various pretty green plantings.
www.hudsonriverpark.org

Intrepid Sea-Air-Space Museum ❷ 1I

This aircraft carrier turned museum has plenty of military hardware, from high-tech spy planes to the nuclear submarine USS *Growler*, but the best place to grasp the nature and history of the USS *Intrepid* is outside, on the 900-ft (274-m) flight deck, from which aircraft went into battle,

beginning in the darkest days of World War II and last seeing action during the Vietnam War. *Adm. Open 10am-5pm Mon-Fri, 10am-6pm Sat-Sun, Apr-Sep; 10am-5pm Tue-Sun, Oct-Mar. Pier 86, W 46th St and 12th Ave, T: 212 245 0072, http://intrepidmuseum.org*

The Jewish Museum ❷ 3M

Explores 4,000 years of Jewish heritage through painting, sculpture and decorative arts. *Adm. Open 11am-5.45pm Sat-Tue, 11am-5.45pm Fri-Tue, 11am-8pm Thu, closed Wed. 1109 Fifth Ave at 92nd St, T: 212 423 3200, www.thejewishmuseum.org*

The High Line ❶ 2E-1G

An elevated rail line, long abandoned and weed-strewn, has been reborn as an urban park with

Pizza Tours

Pizza was not invented in New York, but it has certainly found a home here. Scott Weiner is a passionate pizza geek and local food historian and his fun, fascinating 'Scott's Pizza Tours' chase the city's best pizzas on walking or riding tours. *T: 212 913 9903, www.scottspizzatours.com*

Lincoln Center for the Performing Arts ❷ 2J

The world's largest performing arts center is home to 12 resident arts organizations representing the highest standards of excellence in symphony, opera, chamber music, theater, dance, film and arts education *(see p.31)*. *65th and Columbus Ave, T: 212 875 5456, www.lincolncenter.org*

Lower East Side ❶ 5D-6D

Low-rise and densely inhabited, this downtown 'Gateway to America' has accommodated wave after wave of

Visitors flock to the Metropolitan Museum of Art

immigrants, from the first Irish, Germans, East European Jews and Italians to today's Asians, Latinos and Puerto Rican 'Loisadas'. Though gentrification has brought hipster bars, boutiques and clubs, reminders of the 19th-century immigrant experience remain at historic landmarks such as the Eldridge Street Synagogue, delis like Katz's *(see p.42)*, or the fascinating Tenement Museum, a collection of original tenement buildings which, from 1863 to 1935, housed thousands of people from 20 nations. **Tenement Museum**: *Viewable by guided tour only, book in advance. 103 Orchard St at Delancey St, T: 212 982 8420, http://tenement.org*

Madison Square Garden ❶ 2G

Madison Square Garden hosts more than 300 events a year, but it's best known as the home of the NY Knicks (*see p.37*) (basketball) and the NY Rangers (hockey). Almost any kind of indoor activity that draws large audiences can be held here, from political conventions to top rock and pop concerts. *31st to 33rd St and Seventh Ave, T: 212 465 6741, www.thegarden.com*

Metropolitan Museum of Art ❷ 3L

Two million works of art from every corner of the globe; showstoppers include the Egyptian Temple of Dendur, in a glass-walled gallery of its own, the American Wing, and African, European, photographic, and 20th-century art collections. Explore the Roof Garden, with its seasonal exhibitions, and admire the views of Central Park and surrounding skyscrapers. *Adm (includes entry to the Cloisters, see p.6). Open 9.30am- 5.30pm Tue-Thu & Sun, 9.30am-9pm Fri-Sat. 1000 Fifth Ave at 82nd St, T: 212 535 7710, www.metmuseum.org*

MoMA ❷ 3I

Yoshio Tanaguchi's spacious reworked galleries combine with the original architecture to provide a stunning exhibition space for an awe-inspiring modern art collection. Its cinema has a roster of 22,000 films, while the alfresco sculpture garden is a great place for weary souls to pass a quiet half hour. *Adm. Open 10.30am-5.30pm Wed-Mon and until 8pm Fri. 11 W 53rd St, btw Fifth & Sixth Ave, T: 212 708 9400, www.moma.org*

Morgan Library & Museum ❶ 4H

This is one of the best collections in the world of rare and exceptional books and works of art, all gathered by J. Pierpont Morgan. Manuscripts from around the globe include Ancient Egyptian scripts, right through to the scribbles of Bob Dylan's 'Blowin' in the Wind'. A 2006 extension by Renzo Piano has enhanced this handsome museum, financier Morgan's 19th-century home. *Adm. Open 10.30am-5pm Tue-Thu, 10.30am-9pm Fri (free 7pm-9pm), 10am-6pm Sat,*

Museum of Modern Art (MoMA)

11am-6pm Sun. 225 Madison Ave at 36th St, T: 212 685 0008, www.themorgan.org

The Museum at FIT ❶ 2G

With more big-name designers than on the catwalk, this is one of the most comprehensive hoards of 20th-century fashions in the world. Armani, Chanel and Dior labels mix in with ever-changing displays on textiles, jewelry and fashion photography. *Open 12noon-8pm Tue-Fri, 10am-5pm Sat, closed Sun-Mon. Seventh Ave at 27th St, T: 212 217 4558, www.fitnyc.edu/museum*

New-York Historical Society ❷ 2L

Artifacts and relics from the American past, including Tiffany lamps, dollhouses, death masks, and more. *Open 10am-6pm Tue-Sat, 11am-5.45pm Sun. 2 W 77th St, at Central Park West, T: 212 873 3400, www.nyhistory.org*

New York Public Library ❶ 3H

Two huge seated lions, named Patience and Fortitude, flank the main entrance of this classic 1911 beaux-arts building. Through the bronze entrance doors, you enter an enormous white-marble-filled atrium with a monumental staircase. Take a moment to enjoy the elaborate ceiling frescos in the grand third-floor Rose Main Reading Room, and don't miss the ornately decorated stuccos in its vestibule. *Open 10am-6pm Mon & Thu-Sat, 10am-8pm Tue-Wed. 455 Fifth Ave at 40th St, T: 917 275 6975, www.nypl.org*

Studying in New York Public Library

Rockefeller Center & Radio City ❷ 3I

At the heart of this beautiful art deco mini-city is Rockefeller Plaza's famous outdoor ice rink (in winter only) with its golden statue of Prometheus, and soaring 30 Rock, its lobby painted with murals. Take a behind-the-scenes tour of the NBC Studios or marvel at the jewel-like Radio City Music Hall, New York's dazzling art deco masterpiece and, when it opened in 1932, the largest theater in the world. For some of the best views of NYC visit the Top of the Rock observation deck at 30 Rockefeller Plaza. **NBC**: *30 Rockefeller Plaza, 49th St, T: 212 664 3700*. **Radio City**: *Sixth Ave at 50th St, T: 212 247 4777*. **Top of the Rock**: *Open 8am-12midnight daily (last elevator 11pm), T: 212 698 2000, www.rockefellercenter.com, www.topoftherocknyc.com*

SoHo Cast-Iron District ① 3D-4D

The chic and beautiful flock here for the designer shopping (see p.21) – Stella McCartney, Versace – but the

South Street Seaport

historic district is also a glittering architectural gem featuring the best examples of 19th-century cast-iron in the US. Beginning in the 1970s, the abandoned warehouse buildings were converted into studios by a coterie of artists and sculptors.

South Street Seaport ① 4B

This historic maritime area and mall boasts 100 shops, restaurants and cafés and is a lovely area to spend the day. There is also a fleet of vintage ships, schooners and tugboats. *Pier 17 mall open 10am-9pm Mon-Sat, 11am-8pm Sun (bars and restaurants open later). East River at Fulton St, T: 212 732 8257, www.southstreetseaport.com*

Statue of Liberty

Statue of Liberty & Ellis Island Immigration Museum ① 1A

Take the Circle Line ferry to the icon that welcomed 12 million newcomers to America from 1892 to 1954. A gift from the people of France, Liberty weighs 312,000 lbs (141,500 kg), her pointed finger is 8 ft (2.4 m) long and her 22-story steel frame was built by Gustave Eiffel. You'll need advance

Guided tours are available at the United Nations building

reservations to access the crown (www.statuecruises.com). You can also take a ferry ride to Ellis Island where, at the turn of the 20th century and up until 1954, immigrants arrived into NY. Ferries leave from Battery Park to Liberty Island and Ellis Island approx every 30 minutes 8.30am-4.30pm. *T: 1 877 523 9849, www.statuecruises.com.* **Staute of Liberty**: *www.nps.gov/stli.* **Ellis Island**: *www.nps.gov/elis*

United Nations ❷ 5I

The imposing buildings of the UN's headquarters were designed by Swiss architect Le Corbusier and have been newly refurbished. Inside the monolithic tower, some of the most important decisions in modern political history concerning human rights, economic development and peacekeeping missions have been disputed and agreed. Guided tours give information on the history of the UN, as well as displays of art from member states and temporary exhibitions on pertinent affairs. *Adm. Tours run 9.45am-4.45pm Mon-Fri (-4.15pm Sat-Sun; weekends closed Jan & Feb). Closed public holidays. First Ave & 46th St, T: 212 963 8687, www.un.org/tours*

Washington Square Park ❶ 3E

Surrounded by New York University in the heart of Greenwich Village, the park buzzes with activity, especially in the summer. Street artists, buskers and musicians perform to interested passers-by, while the wide green lawns and benches are an excellent place for a spot of people-watching or relaxing. The iconic Washington Square Arch, central fountain, statues and chess tables make this the ideal hangout or place for a walk. At the foot of Fifth Ave. *www.washingtonsquarepark.org*

Whitney Museum ❶ 2E

Edward Hopper's wife donated his entire collection of life's work to the Whitney; the unusual 1960s concrete square contains 2,500 of his works.

Washington Square is a popular hangout

The Whitney displays and promotes solely 20th-century American photography, art, sculpture and print, with world-class pieces by Rothko, Man Ray and Andy Warhol.

The museum has recently moved to a Renzo Piano-designed downtown location next to the High Line. *Adm. Open 11am-6pm Wed-Thu, 1pm-9pm Fri, 11am-6pm Sat-Sun. 999 Gansevoort St, T: 212 570 3600, http://whitney.org*

9/11 Memorial & Museum ❶ 3B

The memorial site opened on September 12, 2011 and consists of two vast, reflecting pools where waterfalls cascade on all sides within the original footprints of the Twin Towers. The memorial pools are inscribed with the names of those who died in 2001. The 9/11 museum opened 3 years later on the 9/11 anniversary and tells the story of events on that fateful day. Tickets, which give entrance to both the memorial and the museum, can be reserved online for a specific date and time up to 3 months before your visit. A moving photography exhibition can also be found further uptown at the Ground Zero Museum Workshop (❶ 2F) where tours take you on a journey through Marlon Suson's aftermath photos of this tragic event in history in his capacity as the official Ground Zero photographer for the Uniformed Firefighters Association. *Adm (free entrance on Tues from 5pm to close). Entrance at intersections: Liberty & Greenwich Sts, Liberty & West Sts, and West & Fulton Sts. Memorial open 7.30am-9pm daily. Museum open 9am-8pm Sun-Thur, 9am-9pm Fri & Sat, T: 212 268 2000, www.911memorial.org*

Rooftop NY

When the cocktail hour rolls around, the city's most fabulous head to rooftop bars for trendy drinks and drop-dead sunset views. Especially hot is Tequila Park at the Hudson Hotel (❷ 2J/❹, *356 W 58th St at 10th Ave, www.hudsonhotel.com*); another favorite is the Salon de Ning at the Peninsula Hotel, ❷ 3J, with its stunning views over Fifth Avenue and Midtown Manhattan (*700 Fifth Av at 55 St, www.peninsula.com*).

Manhattan Bridge at night: connecting Lower Manhattan with Brooklyn

new york places to shop

The city is a shopper's paradise. From *haute couture*, to antiques, to original artworks and retro collectibles, you'll find everything here. If you crave the latest designer brands and don't mind paying 'retail', head for the chi-chi boutiques of Madison Avenue or the storied department stores along Fifth Avenue. If high-end items at bargain prices are your thing, and you enjoy the thrill of the hunt, then make a beeline for such tried-and-true cut-price emporiums as Century 21 and Loehmann's.

buy it places to shop

Areas

Chelsea, West Village & the Meatpacking District ❶ 2E-2F

With near-daily fashion photo shoots lighting up streets of cobblestone, this historic area mixes high and low. Here you'll find all-American staples such as Gap and Banana Republic as well as jewel-box boutiques, art galleries, and the chic flagship stores of top designers such as Alexander McQueen (*417 W 14th St, T: 212 645 1797*) and Diane von Furstenberg (*874 Washington St, T: 646 486 4800*).

Chinatown ❶ 4B-4C

New York's Chinatown is a mecca for traditional Chinese paper lanterns, toys, and fans, slippers, hand-carved mah-jong sets, as well as art supplies, cut-price scarves and fake designer bags and watches.
www.explorechinatown.com

East Village & Lower East Side ❶ 5E

Gentrification has tried to tame Manhattan's punk-rock bohemian heart. But its unruly self pops up in places such as the neighborhood's main drag, St Mark's Place, with its tattoo parlors, alternative record and bookshops, and kitsch emporiums. Head east along Ninth Street for the city's top vintage clothing shops.

Entrance to Saks on Fifth Avenue

Fifth Avenue sign

Fifth Avenue ❶ 3E/❷ 3P

NY's glitziest shopping street is a jaw-dropping spectacle of over-the-top consumerism. The classic stores are here: Saks Fifth Avenue (*see p.24*), Henri Bendel, Bergdorf Goodman, Cartier, Lord & Taylor (*see p.23*) and Tiffany & Co., not to mention the US flagships of big international brands such as H&M, Zara, and Uniqlo.

Flatiron District ❶ 3F-3G

Originally known as 'Ladies' Mile' for its lineup of elegant turn-of-the-century department stores, lower Sixth Avenue is now home to discount chains. The stretch of Broadway and Fifth Avenue from 14th St to the wedge-shaped Flatiron Building at 23rd St has had a second lease of life with the arrival of such flagship stores as ABC Carpet and Paul Smith.

Madison Avenue & 57th St ❶ 3G/❷ 3P

With its fabled art galleries, expensive antique stores, and chic designer boutiques (Armani, Burberry, Calvin Klein, Chanel, Chloé, Etro, Jimmy Choo, Dior, Gaultier, Gucci, Valentino, YSL), this may be Manhattan's most exclusive shopping nexus. Make detours east for Bloomingdale's and north to museum stores along Fifth Avenue's Museum Mile.

SoHo & NoLiTa ❶ 3C/4D

Shop till you drop at SoHo's wall-to-wall designer boutiques (agnès b, Daryl K, Anna Sui, Yamamoto) and major-brand stores (J Crew, Topshop, French Connection) or strut your stuff in NoLiTa, the trendy little shopping district just east of SoHo, bursting with clothing boutiques selling downtown fashions and chic shoes (Eva, Matta, Sigerson Morrison).

The sharp end of the Flatiron Building

Tax Max!
Clothing and shoe purchases under $110 are exempt from city and state taxes. The standard sales tax of 8.875% is applied to purchases of $110 and higher purchases.

Upper West Side ❷ 1L-1M

Standing tall with 50 high-end retailers, the Time Warner Center welcomes you in to the Upper West Side. Always just a short walk away from a picnic in Central Park, the area is home to a more varied mix of peoples than you might find anywhere in the world. The residents here know where to find the best gourmet food, most stylish home accents and top world wines. And they aren't afraid to tell you – if you ask.

Greenwich Village ❶ 2E

Tucked into niches and corners of this historic low-rise neighborhood you'll find clothing boutiques, accessories and jewelry stores, gifts and books. Also keep an eye out for antiques and vintage clothing.

Book Stores

Barnes & Noble

With six big stores dotted around Manhattan (and two in Brooklyn), you are usually not far from getting your Barnes & Noble book fix. This chain bookstore stocks a large and varied range of titles and hosts related events in all its stores. www.bn.com

Strand Bookstore ❶ 4E

The largest of the remaining independent bookstores, the Strand is known for its mind-blowing selection of new, used and rare books. It boasts '18 Miles of Books' but it feels like much more. Also hosts events. *828 Broadway at 12th St, T: 212 473 1452, www.strandbooks.com*

Three Lives & Co. ❶ 3E

This is the quintessential Village bookstore; small and hushed and packed to the rafters with books. *154 W 10th St btw Sixth and Seventh Ave, T: 212 741 2069, http://threelives.com*

Candy Stores

Dylan's Candy Bar ❷ 4J

The estate-sized candy boutique owned by Dylan Lauren, Ralph's daughter, boasts creative and delicious creations beyond your wildest dreams. *1011 3rd Ave btw 60th & 61st Sts, T: 646 735 0078, www.dylanscandybar.com*

Economy Candy ❶ 5D

A floor-to-ceiling sugar rush that stocks classic treats like kingsize sweetie necklaces and giant swirly lollies. At the front are trays of hand-dipped chocolates sold by the piece. *108 Rivington St btw Essex & Ludlow Sts, T: 212 254 1531, www.economycandy.com*

Department Stores

Barneys New York ❷ 3J

Style nirvana: Barneys' flagship store sells sleek and chic designer fashions, smart accessories, killer shoes, and unique children's clothes. Its annual Christmas windows entice and shock passers-by with cutting-edge displays. *660 Madison Ave at 61st St, T: 212 826 8900, www.barneys.com*

Bergdorf Goodman ❷ 3J/❹
Founded around the turn-of-the-century, Bergdorf sells luxury clothing for the upscale urban fashionista. *754 Fifth Ave at 58th St, T: 212 753 7300, www.bergdorfgoodman.com*

Bloomingdale's ❶ 4D/❷ 4J/❹
This art deco landmark sells the latest fashion trends, not to mention vast stocks of housewares, bedding,

and gifts. A second location on lower Broadway caters to a hip, young clientele. *1000 Third Ave at 59th St, T: 212 705 2000.* **Branch:** *504 Broadway btw Spring and Broome Sts, T: 212 729 5900, www.bloomingdales.com*

Jeffrey ❶ 2F
Stylish and minimalist: Jeffrey sells new-wave designer clothes with an emphasis on to-die-for footwear. *449 W 14th St btw Ninth Ave & 10th*

Ave, T: 212 206 1272, https://jeffreynewyork.com

Lord & Taylor ❶ 3H
Open since 1826, this department store carries popular classics at mid-range prices. *424 Fifth Ave, T: 212 391 3344, www.lordandtaylor.com*

Macy's ❶ 3H
Macy's bustling flagship store is said to be the largest in the world. Each year Macy's hosts the Thanksgiving

Macy's department store

Day Parade (*see p.61*) with marching bands, balloons and floats making their way through the city. *151 W 34th St btw Broadway & Seventh Ave, T: 212 695 4400, www.macys.com*

Pearl River ❶ 4D

This big, colorful Chinese department store sells shellfulls of brightly colored slippers, lanterns, cheongsam, woks and chopsticks. *477 Broadway, T: 212 431 4770, www.pearlriver.com*

Saks Fifth Avenue ❷ 3I

A wonderfully elegant store, Saks is known for its outstanding service. The best of European and American designers is sold throughout its US stores; New York is the original. *611 Fifth Ave, T: 212 753 4000, www.saksfifthavenue.com*

Designer Discount

Century 21 ❶ 3B

Calling itself 'New York's Best Kept Secret', this humongous designer store has all the essentials. A treasure trove of bargains, the trade-off is queuing, barging, and communal changing rooms. *22 Cortlandt St, T: 212 227 9092, www.c21stores.com*

INA ❶ 3D

Sought-after designer outfits, some straight from the runway, can be found at knock-down prices in boutique shops. *Six locations including 101 Thompson St, T: 212 941 4757, www.inanyc.com*

Loehmann's ❶ 3F

At up to 75% off top designer labels, the store is full of finds. Check the renowned Back Room for the best of the best. *101 Seventh Ave at 16th St, T: 212 352 0856, www.loehmanns.com*

Electronics

Apple Store ❷ 3J & ❶ 3D

Accessories for your iPod and a plethora of white desirables from Apple. *Open 24 hrs. Five Manhattan locations including 767 Fifth Ave,*

Sales

Unlike European stores, New York shops run sales for every occasion, from Valentine's Day to Veteran's Day. Check local newspapers for details or sign up for store e-mails and discount coupons. For current sales activity (including deeply discounted designer sample sales), visit sites such as *www.dailycandy.com* and *www.topbutton.com*

T: 212 336 1440; 72 Greene St, T: 212 226 3126, www.apple.com/retail

B&H ● 2G
The country's largest camera and video equipment superstore, all at competitive prices. This electronic mecca has everything from digital SLRs to full-size telescopes and plenty of secondhand equipment on the second floor. *Closed Sat. 420 9th Ave at 34th St, T: 212 444 6615, www.bhphotovideo.com*

Household

Fishs Eddy ● 3F
A fun store to shop for vintage and retro dinner and glassware. *889 Broadway at 19th St, T: 212 420 9020, www.fishseddy.com*

John Derian Company ● 4E
This charming store was built around John Derian's classic decoupage plates but now includes terra-cotta pottery, Parisian candleholders, and other objets d'art. *6 E 2nd St btw Second Ave and the Bowery, T: 212 677 3917, www.johnderian.com*

> **Electronic Tips**
> Electronic, musical, and photographic equipment can be good value. Check for compatibility issues, then make your purchases from reliable outlets such as B&H, J&R Music World, Best Buy or department stores.

Lost City Arts ● 4E
20th-century design classics and urban ephemera: mail boxes, gas pumps, and shop signs. Recognized internationally as a leading source of modern designer furniture, lighting and accessories. *18 Cooper Square, nr Bowery, T: 212 375 0500, www2.lostcityarts.com*

MoMA Design Store ● 3I & ● 4D
Wonderful and original items inspired by the museum's (see p.11) 20th-century art collection. **Branches**: 44 W 53rd St at Fifth Ave, T: 212 767 1050; 81 Spring St at Crosby St, T: 646 613 1367, www.momastore.org

Lingerie

La Petite Coquette ● 3E
Tiny lingerie boutique with everyday favorites as well as rare brands: caters to celebs and native West Villagers. *51 University Place btw Ninth & 10th Sts, T: 888 473 5799, www.thelittleflirt.com*

Markets

The Antiques Garage ● 3G
The huge flea market is filled with funky junk, from pocket watches to pre-World War I bags. *Open 9am-5pm Sat & Sun. 112 W 25th St btw Sixth & Seventh Aves, T: 212 243 5343, www.hellskitchenfleamarket.com*

Chelsea Market ● 2F
Huge indoor market with loads of different retailers selling wines, cheeses, meats and flowers. Enjoy the ground-floor cafés, with free Wi-Fi access (see p.55). *Open 7am-9pm Mon-Sat, 8am-8pm Sun. 75 Ninth Ave btw 15th &16th Sts, http://chelseamarket.com*

A vibrant NY flower market

Eataly ❶ 3G

This sprawling Italian marketplace has everything for the gourmet shopper, from pastas to gelato to pastries to beers, and you can dine in at one of several chic eateries (*see p.44*). Open 10am-11pm Mon-Sun. *200 Fifth Ave btw 23rd & 24th Sts, T: 212 229 2560, www.eataly.com*

Essex Street Market ❶ 5D

This gourmet market dates from 1940 but offers some of the most thrilling, cutting-edge food in town from a handful of the city's top food vendors. *Open 8am-7pm Mon-Sat, 10am-6pm Sun. 75 Ninth Ave btw 15th & 16th Sts, T: 212 312 3603, www.essexstreetmarket.com*

Hell's Kitchen Flea Market ❶ 2H

This vibrant outdoor market includes vendors from The Annex, (formerly located in Chelsea). Expect antiques, collectibles, vintage clothing and much much more. *39th W St btw 9th & 10th Aves, T: 212 243 5343, www.hellskitchenfleamarket.com*

Union Square Greenmarket ❶ 4F

Fabulous farmers' market selling everything from herbs, gourds and potted cacti to organic veggies, wild boar and Amish cheeses, with stockpiles of freshly baked breads. *Open 8am-6pm Mon, Wed, Fri & Sat. Union Square, Broadway at 14th St, T: 212 788 7476, www.cenyc.org*

Top Designer Boutiques

John Varvatos ❶ 4D

Standing on the former site of the iconic CBGB, Mr. Varvatos has created a slick simulacrum of the old club to sell $250 shirts and $2,000 jackets. A section of CBGB's wall, covered in band fliers, has been preserved under glass. *315 Bowery, T: 212 358 0315, www.johnvarvatos.com*

Kirna Zabete ❶ 3D

Fashionistas shop here for clothes and accessories by superstar designers; now in a bigger location on Broome St. *96 Green St btw Greene & Wooster Sts, T: 212 941 9656, www.kirnazabete.com*

Kisan Concept Store ❶ 3D

Selling beautifully curated high-street women's and children's wear, Kisan moves the merchandise with serious sales. *125 Greene Sts btw Houston & Prince Sts, T: 212 475 2470, https://kisanstore.com*

Opening Ceremony ❶ 4C

Set up by co-founders Humberto Leon and Carol Lim 11 years ago. In this gallery-cum-showroom discover the coolest indie labels from the US, Europe and Asia. *35 Howard St at Crosby St, T: 212 219 2688, www.openingceremony.us*

Toys

FAO Schwarz ❷ 3J/❹

NY's most manic toy shop, check out the monster-sized stuffed toys. On entering, you're greeted by a singing three-story clocktower. *767 Fifth Ave at 58th & 59th Sts, T: 212 644 9400, www.fao.com*

Playing Mantis ❶ 3C

A magical place selling innovative toys fashioned with natural materials,

Colorful interior of Marmalade Vintage

many hand-hewn. *32 N Moore St at btw Varick & Hudson Sts, T: 646 484 6845, www.playing-mantis.com*

Toys 'R' Us ❷ 3I

This Times Square location is sure to impress with its 60-foot (80-metre) ferris wheel, roaring dinosaur, giant Barbie townhouse and a Candyland you'll never forget. *1514 Broadway at 44th St, T: 646 366 8800, www.toysrusinc.com*

Vintage Clothes

Allan & Suzi ❶ 4D

You may bump into a celeb or two when shopping at this new and vintage designer clothing store. Owners Allan and Suzi have dressed an impressive list of stars over the years. Great for vintage shoes and jewellery too. *237 Centre St btw Grand St & Broome St, T: 212 724 7445, http://allanandsuzi.net*

Edith Machinist ❶ 5D

Although known for its bags and accessories, this Lower East Side

Personal Shopper
Want a peek at fabulous 'insider' sales? The Shop Gotham's Garment Center tour is a three-hour shop-till-you-drop excursion that is sure to yield true bargains. *T: 212 209 3370, www.shopgotham.com*

shop has a huge selection of vintage clothes and shoes. *104 Rivington St at Ludlow St, T: 212 979 9992, www.edithmachinist.com*

Marmalade Vintage ❶ 4D

For some amazing vintage finds head make a beeline here. *174 Mott St, T: 212 473 8070, www.marmaladevintage.com*

Resurrection ❶ 4D

Vintage store specialising in haute designers (Yves St. Laurent, Halston, Alaia, Gucci) and pre-psychedelic '60s, glam rock '70s and decadent '80s gear. *217 Mott St nr Spring St, T: 212 625 1374, www.resurrectionvintage.com*

new york entertainment

The city's cinemas, concert halls, jazz and rock clubs, comedy clubs, nightclubs and bars pulse with activity. From ground-breaking dance performances to Broadway theater spectaculars, New York leads the world. Hundreds of performances are staged for free, including street festivals and film and opera in the park. To keep abreast of what's hot and what's not, ask a New Yorker, consult the internet, or check the listings in local magazines and newspapers, including *New York magazine*, *Time Out New York*, the *New York Times* and *The New Yorker*. For standby tickets on the day of a performance, hit the TKTS booth in Times Square. Tickets for baseball and football games are like gold dust, but the city offers plenty of other sporting opportunities, as spectator or participant.

watch it entertainment

Tickets

For the best deals, first try the box office, where last-minute discounts are often available. Check out sites such as www.playbill.com and www.broadwaybox.com for special promotions (such as theater tickets plus dinner). Tickets to Broadway shows, concerts and sports events can also be purchased from brokers such as:

Telecharge

T: 212 239 6200, www.telecharge.com
(theater and concerts)

Ticketmaster

T: 212 307 4100, www.ticketmaster.com
(theater, concerts, sporting events).

TKTS ❷ 2I, ❶ 4B

For 20%-50% discounts on same-day performances.
Times Square: open 3pm-8pm Mon & Wed-Sat, 2pm-8pm Tue, and 3pm Sun for evening tickets. For matinees: 10am-2pm Wed & Sat, 11am-3pm Sun. W 47th St & Broadway.
T: 212-912-9770;

South Street Seaport: (see p.13) open 11am-6pm Mon-Sat, 11am-4pm Sun. Corner of Front & John Sts, www.tdf.org

Cinema

New York is a film lover's paradise for new releases, classic and foreign films. T: 212 777 3456 (FILM), www.moviefone.com

Angelika Film Center ❶ 4D

Art films, with quality coffee and cake. 18 W Houston St at Mercer St, T: 212 995 2570, http://angelikafilmcenter.com

Landmark Sunshine Cinema ❶ 4D

Restored vaudeville theater with five screens. 143 E Houston St btw First & Second Aves, T: 212 260 7289, www.landmarktheaters.com

AMC Loews Lincoln Square 13 ❷ 2K

Thirteen screens, including an eight-story 3D screen showing latest releases in IMAX 3-D. 1998 Broadway at 68th St, T: 212 336 5020, www.amctheatres.com

HBO Bryant Park Summer Film Festival

HBO Bryant Park Summer Film Festival

Sit under the stars at the free Bryant Park Film Festival, where flicks are shown on Mondays on a huge screen: take a blanket, a hamper and your dreams. Sixth Ave btw 40th & 42nd Sts, T: 212 512 5700, www.bryantpark.org

TKTS ticket booth on Times Square

The Paris ❷ 3J

An elegant post-war movie house icon. *4 W 58th St, T: 212 688 3800, www.theparistheatre.com*

Classical Music

Bargemusic ❶ 5B

Hear chamber music performed by top international players in a 102-foot (31-metre) barge with the lower Manhattan skyline as a backdrop. *Fulton Ferry Landing, Brooklyn, T: 718 624 2083, www.bargemusic.org*

Courtyard of the Lincoln Center

Carnegie Hall ❷ 3J/❹

The Carnegie Hall, the small Weill Recital Hall and the state-of-the-art Zankel Hall offer chamber music concerts, recitals and full orchestral extravaganzas. *154 W 57th St at Seventh Ave, T: 212 247 7800, www.carnegiehall.org*

Lincoln Center ❷ 2J/❹

The massive arts complex (*see p.10*) includes the world-famous Metropolitan Opera, Alice Tully Hall (used for chamber music and recitals) and the David H. Koch Theater, home of the New York City Ballet. Following a 50th-anniversary multimillion-dollar renovation, the centre boasts a new atrium and an external makeover with plaza walkways, an urban grove and revitalized water fountain. *65th St at Columbus Ave, T: 212 875 5456, http://lc.lincolncenter.org*

St Thomas Church ❷ 3I/❹

Check the website for the calendar of concerts and recitals at this French-Gothic church. *1 W 53rd St at Fifth Ave, T: 212 757 7013, www.saintthomaschurch.org*

Shakespeare in the Park

Stand in (very long) lines for free tickets to the open-air summer productions at the Delacorte Theater; tickets go on sale at 1pm. A limited number are available by logging on to the website at midnight before each day's show. *T: 212 967 7555, www.shakespeareinthepark.org*

watch it

Be on TV
The easiest way to get tickets for the many shows that are taped in New York is to check out these websites:
http://gonyc.about.com and
http://talkshows.about.com

Clubs &
Lounge Bars

For dance halls with VIP rooms to sports bars and supper clubs, check magazines such as *Time Out*, *New York magazine*, *Details*, *Paper magazine*, *CITY* or gay listings in HX.

40/40 ❶ 3G
Owned by Jay-Z, 40/40 is a hyper-chic sports bar and lounge.
6 W 25th St, T: 212 832 4040,
http://the4040club.com

Bemelmans Bar ❷ 4L
This art deco bar offers a classy backdrop to enjoy a little jazz trio.
35 E 76th St, T: 212 744 1600,
www.thecarlyle.com

32

Butterfield 8 ❶ 3H
Retro lounge bar with leather banquettes and comfort food.
5 E 38th St btw Fifth & Madison Ave,
T: 212 679 0646,
www.butterfield8nyc.com

Gaslight ❶ 2F
With no cover charge, this small club is always jumpin'. *400 W 14th St at Ninth Ave, T: 212 479 7306,*
www.gaslightnyc.com

Cielo ❶ 2E
Famed for its cutting edge sound system and recipient of numerous club awards; you can't go wrong at this well known and highly respected hot spot. *18 Little W 12th St, btw Ninth Ave and Washington St,*
T: 212 645 5700, www.cieloclub.com

Marquee ❶ 1G
This is a celebrity-magnet featuring hip-hop and house music with big-name DJs. You'll find it easiest to get past the velvet rope close to opening time at 11pm. *289 Tenth Ave, T: 646 473 0202,*
http://marqueeny.com

Comedy &
Cabaret

Caroline's on Broadway ❷ 2I/❹
Widely regarded as the top comedy club in the US. *1626 Broadway,*
T: 212 757 4100, www.carolines.com

Comic Strip ❷ 4L
Stand-up with up to 15 comedians a night, including an occasional appearance by Eddie Murphy, who started out here, as did Jerry Seinfeld. *1568 Second Ave btw 81st & 82nd Sts, T: 212 861 9386, www.comicstriplive.com*

Duplex ❶ 3E
New York's oldest piano bar; a fun-packed mix of gay cabaret, comedy and drag, with an open-mic night.
61 Christopher St at Seventh Ave,
T: 212 255 5438, www.theduplex.com

Gotham Comedy Club ❶ 3F
Well-established club featuring both new and well-known comedians.
208 W 23rd St btw Seventh & Eighth Aves, T: 212 367 9000,
http://gothamcomedyclub.com

Come to Duplex for cabaret and comedy

Dance

New York is a world-renowned showcase for every kind of dance, from classical ballet to avant-garde.

American Ballet Theater ② 2K
Based at the Lincoln Center's Metropolitan Opera House (*see p.31*) in the spring: repertoire ranges from 19th-century classics to modern pieces. *Metropolitan Opera House, Lincoln Center, T: 212 477 3030, www.abt.org*

Joyce Theater ① 2F
The Joyce puts on a variety of different dance genres from modern ballet, jazz-tap and ethnic dance such as flamenco presented by touring troupes in this art deco theater. *175 Eighth Avenue at 19th Street, T: 212 691 9740, www.joyce.org*

New York City Ballet ② 2K
Founded by George Balanchine and based at David H. Koch Theater (*see p.31*): with an annual Nutcracker from November (*see p.61*). *Lincoln Center, T: 212 870 5570, www.nycballet.com*

Jazz

Many recent jazz styles started in NY. Most clubs have a cover charge.

Birdland ① 2H/② 2I/④
Reincarnation of Charlie Parker's legendary supper club with a big

The sign outside Birdland

stage, Southern cuisine and a line-up including the Duke Ellington Orchestra and Chico O'Farrill Afro-Caribbean Jazz Big Band. *315 W 44th St, T: 212 581 3080, www.birdlandjazz.com*

Blue Note ① 3E
Showcasing the biggest names in jazz, blues and R&B. *131 W 3rd St btw MacDougal & Sixth Ave, T: 212 475 8592, www.bluenote.net*

Jazz fans outside the Blue Note

Smalls ❶ 2E

Down a narrow stairway, this small subterranean space is an intimate jazz dive. *183 W 10th St, btw Seventh Ave and W 4th St, T: 212 252 5091, www.smallsjazzclub.com*

Village Vanguard ❶ 2E

This 'mecca of hip' has launched a galaxy of names such as Mingus, Monk and the club's Vanguard Jazz Orchestra. *178 Seventh Ave at Perry St, T: 212 255 4037, http://villagevanguard.com*

Rock & Pop

Apollo ❷ 2P

Quintessential Harlem palace, still featuring the Amateur Night where the Jackson Five were discovered. *253 W 125th St, btw Seventh & Eighth Aves, T: 212 531 5300, www.apollotheater.org*

The Bitter End ❶ 3E

Legions of greats, from Bo Diddley to David Crosby, have played the city's oldest rock club; these days the stars

Performing at SOB's

aren't quite so bright, but the atmosphere's authentic. *147 Bleecker St btw Thompson St and LaGuardia Pl, T: 212 673 7030, www.bitterend.com*

Madison Square Garden ❶ 2G

Mega-venue for theater and sport (*see p.11*). *31st to 33rd St and Seventh Ave, T: 212 465 6741, www.thegarden.com*

Mercury Lounge ❶ 5D

East Village rock'n'roll stalwart, with live music nightly. *217 E Houston St, btw Essex & Ludlow Sts, T: 212 260 4700, www.mercuryloungenyc.com*

SOB's ❶ 3D

Laidback showcase for Latin sounds, reggae, salsa, R&B, Trinidad-carnival and zydeco. *204 Varick St at W Houston St, T: 212 243 4940, http://sobs.com*

Theater

A huge New York tradition, from big power productions to experimental theater. Discounted day-of-performance tickets to selected Broadway productions are sold at the TKTS booths in Times Square and South Street Seaport (*www.tdf.org*).

Broadway Shows

Current top shows include Pippin, The Lion King, Matilda, Phantom of the Opera and Mamma Mia!. For tickets, try one of the ticket options at the front of this section (*see p.30*).

Off and Off-Off Broadway

Off-Broadway theaters showcase new plays, musicals and revues, while smaller off-off Broadway venues produce avant-garde work.

Atlantic Theater Co ❶ 2F
Plays by writers from David Mamet's theater workshop. *336 W 20th St btw Eighth & Ninth Aves, Atlantic Stage 2: 330 W 16th St, T: 212 691 5919, http://atlantictheater.org*

La MaMa ❶ 4E
Founded in a tiny basement in 1961 by Ellen Stewart. La MaMa is a bastion a bastion of Off-Off-Broadway theater and the launchpad for the likes of Lanford Wilson, Harvey Fierstein and Sam Shepard. *74a E Fourth St btw Bowery & Second Ave, T: 212 475 7710, http://lamama.org*

Central Park SummerStage
See everything from world music to grand opera at the SummerStage, ❷ 3K, mid-June to mid-August. Be sure to arrive early – no tickets.
For a schedule call: *T: 212 360 2756, www.cityparksfoundation.org/summerstage/*

Public Theater ❶ 4E
Off-Broadway theater founded by Joseph Papp; showcases much of the city's Shakespeare adaptations as well as new interpretations of both classic and contemporary works. *425 Lafayette St btw Fourth St & Astor Pl, T: 212 539 8500, www.publictheater.org*

Bright lights along Broadway

Sport
Baseball

New York Mets
Based at the open-air ballpark Citi Field, which opened in 2009. *123-01 Roosevelt Ave, T: 718 507 8499 (TIXX), http://newyork.mets.mlb.com*

35

⑤ THEATER DISTRICT

Theaters (alphabetical list):

1. Al Hirschfeld
2. Ambassador
3. American Airlines
4. August Wilson
5. Belasco
6. Bernard B. Jacobs
7. Booth
8. Broadhurst
9. Broadway
10. Brooks Atkinson
11. Circle in the Square
12. Cort
13. Duke
14. Ethel Barrymore
15. Eugene O'Neill
16. Gerald Schoenfeld
17. Gershwin
18. Helen Hayes
19. Imperial
20. John Golden
21. Longacre
22. Lunt-Fontanne
23. Lyceum
24. Majestic
25. Marquis
26. Minskoff
27. Mint
28. Music Box
29. Nederlander
30. Neil Simon
31. New Amsterdam
32. New Victory
33. Palace
34. Richard Rodgers
35. Samuel J. Friedman
36. Second Stage
37. Shubert
38. St. James'
39. Stephen Sondheim
40. Studio 54
41. Walter Kerr
42. Westside
43. Winter Garden

Performing Arts Venues

1. Beacon Theatre
2. Carnegie Hall
3. City Center
4. Foxwoods Theatre
5. Frick Collection Music Room
6. Grace Rainey Rogers Audtm.
7. Julliard School
8. Lincoln Center
9. Merkin Concert Hall
10. Radio City Music Hall
11. Roseland Ballroom
12. Town Hall

Manhattan Plaza

Ninth Avenue

Eighth Avenue

Columbus Circle

Broadway

Late Show with David Letterman (Ed Sullivan Theater)

Times Square

Duffy Square

Seventh Avenue

Carnegie Hall

Avenue of the Americas

Central Park

Rockefeller Center
Radio City Music Hall
Rockefeller Plaza

Fifth Avenue

W41st, W42nd, W43rd, W44th, W45th, W46th, W47th, W48th, W49th, W50th, W51st, W52nd, W53rd, W54th, W55th, W56th, W57th, W58th

Central Park South

Manhattan baseball

New York Yankees
The Yankees play out of their home at the new Yankee Stadium, which was built across the street from its older namesake. *River Ave at 161st St, T: 718 293 4300, http://newyork.yankees.mlb.com*

Basketball

New York Knicks ❶ 2G/❹
Madison Square Garden, Seventh Ave at 32nd St, T: 212 465 6741, www.nba.com/knicks

Billiards and Pool

Amsterdam Billiards Union Square ❶ 4F
One of the swishest pool halls in the city, with 25 Brunswick pool tables. *110 E 11th St at Fourth Ave nr Union Sq, T: 212 995 0333, www.amsterdambilliards.com*

Slate Bar & Pool Room ❶ 3F
Seven pool tables, multiple bars and a restaurant. Mon-Fri pool games $7 an hour. *Open 11am-5pm Mon-Thu, 11am-4am Fri-Sun. 54 W 21st St btw Fifth & Sixth Aves, T: 212 989 0096, www.slate-ny.com*

Bowling

Bowlmor Lanes ❶ 3E
Opened in 1938, with 44 glow-in-the-dark lanes. *110 University Place, btw 12th & 13th Sts, T: 212 255 8188, www.bowlmor.com*

Hockey

New York Rangers ❶ 2G
Madison Sq Garden, Seventh Ave at 32nd St, T: 212 465 6741, http://rangers.nhl.com

Sports Village

Chelsea Piers Sports and Entertainment Complex ❶ 1F
This 30-acre (12-hectare) sports village fills four piers along the Chelsea waterfront. Highlights include a golf driving range and an 80,000-square-foot Field House. *Piers 59-62, 17th-23rd St at West Side Hwy, T: 212 336 6666, www.chelseapiers.com*

Direction to Madison Square Garden

new york places to eat and drink

In New York dining out can cost the moon or set you back mere pocket change, and you can do it at any time of the day or night. Whether it's a classic hot dog from a street vendor, an ethnic lunch deal or the most refined of *haute cuisine*, New York serves up countless types of food from around the world. And New Yorkers are passionate about food – awards are even given for the best street food (the 'Vendys'; *http://streetvendor.org*). While trends and crazes can sweep across the city, only the best survive.

taste it places to eat and drink

Price per person

$ cheap (under $20)
$$ inexpensive ($20-30)
$$$ expensive ($30-60)
$$$$ very expensive ($60+)

Asian

Blue Ribbon Sushi $$ ❶ 3D

Simple, zen-style interior and part of the Blue Ribbon restaurant empire. The owners take pride in the freshness of their fish. *119 Sullivan St btw Prince & Spring Sts, T: 212 343 0404, www.blueribbonrestaurants.com*

Dok Suni's $$ ❶ 5E

Authentic Korean restaurant: go for the biblimbop here – strips of beef, veggies and steaming rice served in a bowl along with little dishes of pickles, kimchi and sauces. Cash only. *119 First Ave btw Seventh St & St Mark's Pl, T: 212 477 9506.*

Ippudo $$ ❷ 1I/❹

In a city inundated with top-notch ramen-noodle shops, this is one of the

Sophisticated food in Chinatown

best. It also has an East Village location (65 Fourth Ave). *321 W 51st St, T: 212 974 2500, www.ippudony.com*

Joe's Shanghai $$ ❶ 4C

Joe's serves up the best steamed soup dumplings in town and authentic Shanghainese dishes. *9 Pell St, T: 212 233 8888. www.joesshanghairestaurant.com*

Shun Lee West $$$ ❷ 2J

Chinese *haute cuisine* with an exhaustive Cantonese, Shanghainese and Szechuan menu. *43 W 65th St nr Columbus Ave, T: 212 595 8895, www.shunleewest.com*

Bagels

Ess-a-Bagel $ ❶ 5F

The perfect roll with a hole. *359 First Ave at 21st St, T: 212 260 2252, www.ess-a-bagel.com*

Basque

Txikito $ ❶ 2G

Basque country cuisine and wine are inventively presented in this rustic Chelsea storefront, with offerings like squid ribbons in an onion and pine nut sauce and flash-fried Basque peppers tossed with sea salt. *240 Ninth Ave, T: 212 242 4730, www.txikitonyc.com*

Chinatown Restaurant

Brunch

Bubby's $$ ❶ 3C
Gorgeous American comfort food, served up 24 hours a day (*except closed 12midnight-7am Tue*). 120 Hudson St at N Moore St, T: 212 219 0666, www.bubbys.com

Pastis $$$ ❶ 2E
Happening bistro in the Meatpacking District. Avoid two-hour waits in the evenings and on weekends by coming for weekday brunch or lunch instead. *Open till 3am Fri & Sat.* 9 Ninth Ave at Little W 12th St, T: 212 929 4844, www.pastisny.com

Celebrity Chefs

Babbo $$$$ ❶ 3E
Though Mario Batali has a number of New York restaurants (see www.mariobatali.com), this is one of the best, serving his creative Italian-inspired cuisine. 110 Waverly Pl btw MacDougal St & Sixth Ave, T: 212 777 0303, www.babbonyc.com

Bouley $$$$ ❶ 3C
The flagship restaurant from acclaimed four-star chef David Bouley offers modern French cuisine with Asian inflections. 163 Duane St at Hudson St, T: 212 964 2525, www.davidbouley.com

Daniel $$$$ ❷ 4J
The elegant eponymous flagship of the Manhattan restaurants owned and operated by super-chef Daniel Boulud. For gentler tariffs, check the website for the chef's three other restaurants. 60 E 65th St btw Madison Ave and Park Ave, T: 212 288 0033, www.danielnyc.com

Crisp linen in the dining room at Daniel

Flower-filled dining room at Le Bernardin

Nobu $$$$ ❶ 3C
Famed Japanese restaurant. Can't get a table? Try sister restaurant Nobu Next Door (*T: 212 334 4445*) – it's just as fantastic. 105 Hudson St at Franklin St, T: 212 219 0500, www.noburestaurants.com

Classic Dining

Le Bernardin $$$$ ❷ 3I/❹
New York's best fish - and one of its overall finest restaurants. *The Equitable Building, 155 W 51st St btw Sixth & Seventh Aves, T: 212 554 1515, www.le-bernardin.com*

Keens $$$$ ❶ 3H/❹

A relic from late-19th-century New York, this old-time chophouse serves some of the city's best steaks. *72 W 36th St, T: 212 947 3636, www.keens.com*

Oyster Bar and Restaurant $$$$ ❶ 4H/❹

Don't leave New York without seeing this Guastavino-tiled Grand Central landmark; sample oysters and seafood soups in the clubby Saloon. *Grand Central Terminal, lower level, T: 212 490 6650, www.oysterbarny.com*

The '21' Club $$$ ❷ 3I/❹

This 1929 speakeasy and former writers' haunt is a fun place to marinate in old-school New York. *21 W 2nd St, T: 212 582 7200, www.21club.com*

The famous Oyster Bar at Grand Central Terminal

Delis

Carnegie Deli $$ ❷ 2J/❹

The definitive New York deli serving the biggest pastrami on rye in the city. *854 Seventh Ave at 55th St, T: 212 757 2245, www.carnegiedeli.com*

Katz's $ ❶ 5D

Lower East Side deli where Meg Ryan had her pastrami-on-rye-induced orgasm in When Harry Met Sally. *205 E Houston St at Ludlow St, T: 212 254 2246, http://katzsdelicatessen.com*

Preparing pastrami sandwiches at Katz's

Second Avenue Deli $$ ❶ 4G/❹

This classic New York deli is no longer on Second Avenue but still serves great matzo ball soup and deli favorites. *162 E 33rd St, T: 212 689 9000, www.2ndavedeli.com*

Zabar's $$ ❷ 1L

The legendary foodie paradise, bursting at the seams with a cornucopia of delicacies including bagels with cream cheese and lox – a New York favorite – and cinnamon babka to die for. *2245 Broadway at 80th St, T: 212 496 1234, www.zabars.com*

Dinner for Two

FireBird $$$ ❷ 2I/❹

This Theater District Russian is a romantic spot for blinis and caviar. *365 W 46th St btw Eighth & Ninth Aves, T: 212 586 0244, www.firebirdrestaurant.com*

Minetta Tavern $$$ ❶ 3E

Once a literati hangout for the likes of Hemingway and O'Neill, today's version is still a hot spot, serving up

Classic burger and fries

a host of sophisticated bistro dishes including the famed Black Label burger at $26 a pop! *113 MacDougal St, T: 212 475 3850, www.minettatavernny.com*

One if by Land, Two if by Sea $$$$ ❶ 3E

This 18th-century carriage house is a temple to romance. Dine on classic fare with a New American twist, although beef Wellington with bordelaise sauce is still a signature dish. *17 Barrow St btw W Fourth St & Seventh Ave, T: 212 255 8649, www.oneifbyland.com*

Food Concourses/ Markets

Chelsea Market $-$$ ❶ 2F

Some of the best food vendors in the city occupy a vintage biscuit factory near the High Line. It's your choice – sit down, take out, or choose to picnic on the High Line, with stunning Hudson River views to keep you company. *75 Ninth Ave, btw 15th & 16th Sts, http://chelseamarket.com*

taste it

No Smoking

Smoking has been limited in public places in New York for several years, but now there is a blanket ban in all clubs, bars, cafés, restaurants and public facilities across the city.

Eataly $-$$$ ❶ 4D

Sprawling Italian-food marketplace from Batali and Bastianich, with restaurants, takeout, a rooftop brewery, and much more.
200 Fifth Ave, btw 23rd & 24th Sts, www.eataly.com

Italian

Lupa $$-$$$ ❶ 3D

Expect reasonably priced authentic Italian fare in this communal dining experience. All the stable offerings, such as fresh 'melt in the mouth' pasta, sit comfortably beside the more specialist dishes such as heart and fluke. *170 Thompson St, T: 212 982 5089, www.luparestaurant.com*

Spaghetti al dente at Quartino's

Quartino's $-$$ ❶ 4D

Tasty Italian food made with fresh organic ingredients: olive oil, wine, pizza, pasta and salads. *11 Bleecker St btw Bowery & Elizabeth Sts, T: 212 529 5133, www.quartino.com*

Late Night/ 24 Hour

Balthazar $$$ ❶ 4D

Fiendishly popular and sophisticated Parisian brasserie; reserve well in advance for dinner, or try early mornings or late at night.
7.30am-12midnight Mon-Thu, 7.30am-1am Fri, 8am-1am Sat, 8am-12midnight Sun. 80 Spring St btw Broadway & Crosby Sts, T: 212 965 1414, www.balthazarny.com

Cafeteria $$ ❶ 2F

Open 24 hours 7 days a week, this trendy Chelsea spot is still hot and serves updated versions of American comfort food. *119 Seventh Ave at 14th St, T: 212 414 1717, www.cafeteriagroup.com*

Mexican/ Southwestern

Empellon Cocina $$-$$$ ❶ 5E

Led by precocious James Beard award nominee Alex Stupak, this

24-hour dining

East Villager puts a thrilling spin on tacos and other classic Mexican dishes. *105 First Ave btw 6th & 7th Sts, T: 212 780 0999, http://empellon.com/cocina*

Maya $$$ ❷ 5J

One of the city's top restaurants serving modern Mexican. *1191 First Ave btw 64th & 65th Sts, T: 212 585 1818, www.richardsandoval.com/mayany*

Sandwiches

Porchetta $ ❶ 5E

At this tiny East Village shop, delicious porchetta (slow-roasted pig with crackling) sandwiches and accompaniments such as beans and greens make for a delicious quick and easy meal or picnic to take out. *110 E. Seventh St nr First Ave, T: 212 777 2151, www.porchettanyc.com*

Southern

Melba's $$ ❷ 2O

Melba's American comfort food or fried chicken and waffles with strawberry butter are beloved in Harlem and beyond. *300 W 114th St at Frederick Douglas Blvd, T: 212 864 7777, http://melbasrestaurant.com*

Tasting Menus

Nearly all the top restaurants have a small eats tasting menu, allowing customers to sample a mouth-watering range of delicacies.

Sylvia's $$ ❷ 3P

Eggs any style and smothered chicken, collard greens and sweet potato pie by Harlem's self-proclaimed queen of soul food. *328 Lenox Ave btw 126th & 127th Sts, T: 212 996 2669, www.sylviasrestaurant.com*

Virgil's Real Barbecue $-$$ ❷ 2I/❹

Serving Southern-style barbecue (think barbecued ribs and chicken, brisket and pulled pork) in the heart of Times Square. *152 W 44th St, T: 212 921 9494, www.virgilsbbq.com*

Spanish & Tapas

Solera $$ ❷ 4I/❹

Sun-drenched Spanish and Catalan menu – try the classic paella and

45

tasty tapas – washed down with jugs of fruity sangria or try a glass from the excellent wine and sherry list. *Closed Sun. 216 E 53rd St, T: 212 644 1166, www.solerany.com*

Tertulia $$-$$$ ❶ 3E
Award-winning tapas menu in a sexy Village spot modeled after the cozy cider houses of Spain. *358 Sixth Ave, T: 646 559 9909, http://tertulianyc.com*

Sweet Things

Café Sabarsky $$–$$$ ❷ 3L
Enjoy a rich Sachertorte or a sumptuous strudel in this luxurious

Indulgent cupcakes at Magnolia

evocation of old Vienna. *Neue Galerie, 1048 Fifth Ave at 86th St, T: 212 288 0665.*

Cupcake Café $ ❶ 2H
Almost-too-pretty-to-eat cupcakes generously covered in icings and bright butter cream flowers. *545 Ninth Ave btw 40th & 41st Sts, T: 212 268 9975, www.cupcakecafe-nyc.com*

Fat Witch Bakery $ ❶ 2F
Try the famed original Fat Witch brownie. *Chelsea Market (see p.26), 75 Ninth Ave at 15th St, T: 888 419 4824, www.fatwitch.com*

Magnolia Bakery $ ❶ 2E
On screen, Carrie Bradshaw and her *Sex and the City* friends indulged in the delights of a frosted Magnolia cupcake, which means by rights you should too. *401 Bleecker St at W 11th St, T: 212 462 2572, www.magnoliabakery.com*

Veniero's $ ❶ 4E
Italian patisserie established in 1894, serving the definitive cappuccino as well as divine NY cheesecake or chocolate mousse cake. *342 E 11th St btw First & Second Aves, T: 212 674 7070, www.venierospastry.com*

Tips on Tipping
Most restaurants do not include a service charge. The standard tip is 15%-20% in restaurants (New Yorkers mostly calculate it by doubling the 8.875% sales tax to get a round 18%). In bars, remember to tip the barman $1 a round.

Vegetarian & Health Food

Angelica Kitchen $ ❶ 4E
Longstanding vegan favorite with an ever-changing menu. Mainstays include walnut-lentil pâté and assorted dragon bowls. *300 E 12th St btw First & Second Aves, T: 212 228 2909, http://angelicakitchen.com*

Dirt Candy $$ ❶ 5E
Michelin-starred East Villager serving sophisticated vegetarian dishes. *430 E ninth St, T: 212 228 7732, www.dirtcandynyc.com*

Enjoy organic dishes at Spring Street

Spring Street Natural Restaurant $$ ❶ 4D
For more than 40 years, this sprawling, plant-filled spot has been serving whole natural foods: salads, stir-fries, fish and free-range chicken and more. *62 Spring St at Lafayette, T: 212 966 0290, www.springstreetnatural.com*

Bars
Relaxed

Fanelli's Café ❶ 3D
Vintage bar/restaurant in trendy SoHo. *94 Prince St at Mercer St, T: 212 226 9412.*

The Half King ❶ 1F
A relaxed classic pub owned by two writers and a director in the heart of Chelsea. *505 West 23rd St, T: 212 462 4300, www.thehalfking.com*

White Horse Tavern ❶ 2E
Built in 1880, this watering hole was favored by such literati as Norman Mailer and Anaïs Nin. It is the place where Dylan Thomas drank his

Sip on a martini or two

fabled last 18 shots of whisky. *567 Hudson St and W 11th St, T: 212 989 3956.*

Swank

King Cole Bar ❷ 3J
The glamourous spot where the Bloody Mary was born; its centerpiece is a classic mural by Maxfield Parrish. *The St. Regis Hotel, 2 E 55th St btw Fifth & Sixth Aves, T: 212 753 4500, www.kingcolebar.com*

Hudson Hotel Library Bar ❷ 2J/❹
Retro-style bar with billiards, fireplace, and antique rugs. Beautiful people and beautiful drinks. *356 W 58th St btw Eighth & Ninth Aves, T: 212 554 6217, www.hudsonhotel.com*

new york practical information

Manhattan is 13.4 miles (21.6 km) long and 0.8-2.3 miles (1.3-3.7 km) wide. Fifth Avenue runs down the middle, dividing streets into east and west. Broadway, following an ancient Indian trail, runs diagonally from north to south, slicing up avenues and creating triangular-shaped city blocks as it goes. Subways are the quickest and most efficient way of getting around; trains are fast and frequent, running 24 hours a day on more than 25 routes and 656 miles (1,056 km) of track. Buses are a handy option if you want to see the town; expect leisurely rides on both the north-south 'uptown' and 'downtown' buses and east-west 'crosstown' buses, especially at rush hour. The city is never short on its iconic yellow taxis (over 13,000), but keep in mind that the going can be slow in rush-hour traffic.

know it practical information

Tourist Info

NYC & Co. ❶ 4B, 4C, ❷ 2I

Information on accommodations, sights and entertainment. *Open 8.30am-6pm Mon-Fri, 9am-5pm Sat & Sun. Official NYC Information Center: 810 Seventh Ave at 53rd St.* **Other branches/kiosks:** *Times Square: Seventh Ave btw 46th and 47th Sts; Macy's Herald Square: 151 W 34th St, btw Seventh Ave & Broadway; Chinatown: Canal, Walker & Baxter Sts; City Hall: Broadway at Park Row; T: 212 484 1222, www.nycgo.com*

> ### Unlimited Ride Card
> Available at subway-station vending machines and subway tellers, the Unlimited Ride MetroCard currently gives unlimited rides on subways and buses for seven days for $30. You can also use a Pay-per-Ride MetroCard for unlimited rides on a top-up basis from $5 *(see right)*.

Times Square Information Center ❷ 3I

Broadway discounts, MetroCards etc. 1560 Broadway, T: 212 484 1222, www.timessquarenyc.org

Arriving by Air

New York is served by three airports. Depending on traffic, they are a 30-90-minute taxi-ride into Manhattan. Recorded info: *T: 800 247 7433.*

John F Kennedy (JFK)
T: 718 244 4444, www.panynj.gov/airports/jfk.html

AirTrain JFK

A direct rail line links all terminals to either Howard Beach station for subway A to Manhattan, or to Jamaica Transportation Center for subways E, J and Z and LIRR (Long Island Rail Road) to Penn Station ❶ 2G. Journey takes 35 minutes to Penn Station and fares cost $7.50 with a Pay-per-Ride MetroCard. *www.panynj.gov/airports/jfk-airtrain.html*

JFK Airtrain

Bus

SuperShuttle's blue vans cost $15 to $22 per person and leave JFK every 15 to 30 minutes around the clock daily, offering door-to-door service to Manhattan hotels and landmarks; reservations are not required for airport-to-Manhattan rides. Inquire at the ground transportation desk on arrival. *T: 800 258 3826, www.supershuttle.com*

Taxi

Official yellow medallion taxis charge a flat rate of $52 into the city (plus a state tax surcharge of 50¢ per journey) *(see p.52).*

LaGuardia

T: 718 533 3400, www.panynj.gov/
airports/laguardia.html

Bus

SuperShuttle's blue vans cost $15 to
$22 per person and leave LaGuardia
every 15 to 30 minutes around the
clock daily, offering door-to-door
service to Manhattan hotels and
landmarks; reservations are not
required for airport-to-Manhattan
rides. Inquire at the ground
transportation desk on arrival.
T: 800 258 3826, www.supershuttle.com

Taxi

Taxis charge around $25-$37 (plus
surcharge & tolls) from LaGuardia
into Manhattan.

Newark Liberty

T: 973 961-6000, www.panynj.gov/
airports/newark-liberty.html

AirTrain Newark

Connects every three minutes to NJ
Transit, PATH and Amtrak. The
AirTrain Newark portion is $5.50 but
included in the fare if you buy a NJ

Transit or Amtrak ticket to the
airport. Check with NJ Transit for
train times into Manhattan. T: 888
397 4636, www.panynj.gov/airports/
ewr-airtrain.html

Taxi

Taxis charge $50-$70 (+ $15
surcharge) into town.

Returning to the Airport

Taxis do not offer flat rates to the
airport. Most hotels can arrange for
shuttle transport or a car service.

Getting Around

MetroCards

MetroCards for use on the subway
and buses are available at station

Signal at pedestrian crossing

vending machines. The fare for one
subway or bus ride is $2.50. You can
buy multi-ride MetroCards in
denominations from $3 to $80.
Bonuses are offered for buying
MetroCards of $10 or more as well
as Pay-per-Ride or Unlimited Ride
MetroCards (see box, left). Children
under 44 inches (1.1 m) ride free.
T: 511, http://new.mta.info

Subway

Traveling by subway is the fastest
way of getting around. Trains
run around the clock and there's
air-conditioning in every car
(though not on platforms).
Subway stations are marked above
ground by a green globe (a red
globe indicates the station may
be closed).

Bus

Though New York's buses can be
slow, especially in the rush hours,
they are air-conditioned. The fare is a
flat rate of $2.50 and includes free
transfer from north-south to east-
west bus. Bills are not accepted;
use exact change (10 x 25¢), or a

MetroCard (see p.51), which includes a free transfer from bus to subway, or between buses.

Taxi

Yellow cabs are good value for groups (no more than four passengers). The rate is $2.50 on entry, plus 50¢ for each additional one-fifth mile or 120 seconds when not moving or in slow traffic. A 50¢ state tax surcharge is applied to every journey. Night surcharge of 50¢ between 8pm and 6am; peak hour surcharge of $1.00 between 4pm and 8pm weekdays. Complaints & lost property: T: 212 639 9675.

Trains

Grand Central Terminal ❶ 4H/❹
Metro-North trains to upstate New York and Westchester. T: 511, http://new.mta.info/mnr

Penn Station ❶ 2G/❹
Amtrak trains to cities in US. T: 800 872 7245, www.amtrak.com; LIRR (Long Island Rail Road) T: 511, http://web. mta.info; NJ Transit to New Jersey. T: 973 275 5555, www.njtransit.com

Bicycle Rental

Loeb Boathouse Cycle Hire ❷ 3K
Central Park, T: 212 517 2233, www.thecentralparkboathouse.com

Water taxi

Subway entrance

Banks

Banking hours are generally 9am-5pm Monday-Friday and Saturday mornings. Arrive in NYC with dollars in cash, traveler's checks or pre-loaded travel cards. Most restaurants and stores accept traveler's checks and credit cards; you can obtain cash from ATMs with most Visa and Maestro symbol cards.

Changing Money

Change money at Travelex offices in airports, some branches of Chase bank (call to check) and American Express offices if you carry their card(s).

Disabled Access

Buses are fully accessible to wheelchair users, but the city's subway system isn't yet fully accessible. By law taxis must accept collapsible wheelchairs. All buildings constructed after 1987 provide access for wheelchairs.
Transportation accessibility information. T: 311, www.nyc.gov

Theater Development Fund

The Theater Development Fund (TDF) Accessibility Programs Check were created to increase access for disabled theatergoers. Go the website and click on 'Ticket Services'. T: 212 912 9770, www.tdf.org

Emergencies

If you have a medical emergency, you can find the nearest Hospital Emergency Room in the Yellow Pages Directory or at www.yellowpages.com.

Roosevelt Hospital ❷ 1J

1000 10th Ave at 59th St, T: 212 523 4000, www.wehealny.org

DOCS ❶ 3G, 4H

Walk-in clinics. 55 E 34th St btw Madison & Park Aves; 202 W 23rd St at Seventh Ave, T: 212 352 2600.
Police, ambulance and fire: T: 911.

Internet

You'll find Wi-Fi hotspots throughout Manhattan (see p.55) but if you have traveled without an internet-enabled

There is disabled access to all buses

device you can still find internet cafés dotted around the city.

Cyber Café ❷ 2I/❹

Open 8am-11pm Mon-Fri, 11am-11pm Sat-Sun. 250 West 49th St btw Broadway & 8th Av, T: 212 333 4109, www.cyber-cafe.com

Mail

US letters cost 45¢ and postcards 32¢. Overseas letters and postcards cost 85¢-$1.05. Stamps are sold at newsstands, delicatessens and supermarkets as well as post offices.

General Post Office ❶ 2G
Open 24 hrs. 421 Eighth Ave,
T: 800 275 8777, www.usps.com

Pharmacy

CVS
24-hour pharmacy chain with stores throughout Manhattan.
www.cvs.com

Duane Reade
24-hour pharmacy chain.
www.duanereade.com

Skate & Blade

Empire Skate Club ❷ 2K
Group skates for experienced skaters in Central Park on Tuesday nights year round. Meet at 8pm outside *Blades West, 156 West 72nd St btw Columbus & Amsterdam Aves,*
T: 212 787 3911, www.empireskate.org

Telephones

Pay phones are becoming harder to find in the city with the popularity of mobile phones. Local calls from pay phones cost 25¢. For phone calls to another area code, dial 1 plus the area code. For international phone calls, dial 011 followed by the country code. Dial directly from pay phones using credit card, cash, or phone cards available from stores and newsstands.

Directory Assistance
411 (New York City)
1 + area code + **555 1212** (outside New York City).

Call Collect
Dial 0, the area code and number.

Tours

Big Onion
Walking tours take in 25 districts and neighborhoods along with Central Park and Brooklyn Bridge.
T: 888 606 9255, www.bigonion.com

Central Park activities

Liberty Helicopters ❶ 4A

Peer down on the skyscrapers with a variety of tours. *Downtown Heliport, 6 East River Piers, T: 212 967 6464, www.libertyhelicopters.com*

New York Double Decker Bus Tours

Hop-on hop-off bus tours on red double deckers: buy tickets on bus from Times Sq, Rockefeller Center, Central Park S and the Empire State Building. *T: 212 445 0848, www.newyorksightseeing.com*

Scott's Pizza Tours

Roam the city on foot or by bus sampling New York's best pizza. *T: 212 913 9903, www.scottspizzatours.com*

Wi-Fi

There are many free Wi-Fi points all over the city, in all branches of the New York Public Library, hotels, parks, and coffee bars. In addition, the Downtown Alliance provides free access to a number of locations. Go to *www.downtownny.com/programs/free-public-wifi* for a list of sites.

Hop-on hop-off bus tours are an easy way to see the city

Central Park Bicycle Tour ❷ 2J/❹

Two-hour bike tours (free rental). *203 W 58th St at Seventh Ave, T: 212 541 8759, http://centralparkbiketours.com*

Circle Line ❶ 1H

Full island cruises and speedboat rides. *Pier 83, 42nd St at 12th Ave, T: 212 563 3200, www.circleline42.com*

Gray Line of New York ❶ 2H/❹

Huge range of tours available. *777 Eighth Ave at 42nd St, T: 212 445 0848, www.newyorksightseeing.com*

Harlem Spirituals

Soul food and jazz tours in Harlem. *T: 212 391 0900, www.harlemspirituals.com*

directory

Our New York directory has everything you need to get the best out of your stay, with a selection of some of the best hotels in all categories that the city has to offer. On top of that, there's an excellent round-up of events occurring throughout the year, enabling you to choose the best time to experience this happening metropolis. In addition to a section on further reading, there's also a little information on how to speak the lingo like a native New Yorker and feel right at home.

Key to Icons

- ⛴ Room Service
- ⑭ Restaurant
- ⓨ Fully Licensed Bar
- ⛲ En suite Bathroom
- @ Business Centre
- 🏔 Health Centre
- ❄ Air Conditioning
- Ⓟ Parking

Places to stay

New York City has nearly 90,000 hotel rooms, from penthouse stratospheres to reasonable bed and breakfasts. For quiet locations, opt for the Upper East Side, east Midtown, or Gramercy Park; for hip and happening hotels, try west Midtown, SoHo and Chelsea.

Luxury Hotels

Hotel Carlyle $$$$ ❷ 4L

⛴ ⑭ ⓨ ⛲ 🏔 ❄

This is an elegant art deco classic, housing the famous classic with the famous Café Carlyle, Turkish tea rooms, The Carlyle Restaurant, and Bemelmans Bar and Bemelmans Bar. *35 E 76th St btw Madison & Park Aves, T: 212 744 1600, www.thecarlyle.com*

Price per room
$ budget (under $180)
$$ moderate ($180-300)
$$$ expensive ($300-480)
$$$$ deluxe ($480+)

Four Seasons $$$$ ❷ 4J/❹

One of Manhattan's most expensive hotels, designed by I.M. Pei, this is 52 stories high with a classy modern interior. *57 E 57th St btw Park & Madison Aves, T: 212 758 5700, www.fourseasons.com/newyork*

Mandarin Oriental Hotel $$$$ ❷ 2J/❹

Five-star style executed with Asian flair. Each of the 244 rooms has a view of either Central Park or the Hudson River. A world-class spa and gourmet restaurant complete the picture. *80 Columbus Circle, T: 212 805 8800, www.mandarinoriental.com/newyork*

The Peninsula New York $$$$ ❷ 3J

With rooms that feel like swanky apartments, one of the best spas in the city, and a rooftop bar, the Peninsula is luxe deluxe. *700 Fifth Ave at 55th St, T: 212 956 2888, www.newyorkpalace.com*

The Pierre $$$$ ❷ 3J

This sumptuous and newly revitalized art deco skyscraper enjoys far-reaching views over Central Park. *2 E 61st St at Fifth Ave, T: 212 838 8000, www.tajhotels.com/pierre*

Hippest Hotels

Ace Hotel $$-$$$ ❶ 3G

This Seattle transplant has one of the city's most buzzing lobbies and rooms with Pendleton spreads, many complete with vintage furniture and turntables. *20 W 29th St btw Fifth Ave & Broadway, T: 212 679 2222, www.acehotel.com/newyork*

Bowery Hotel $$$$ ❶ 4E

Once known for seedy flophouses housing infamous 'Bowery bums', the Lower East Side is now a trendy neighborhood. The Bowery Hotel is packed with retro glamour and boasts 400-thread-count linens, sunken tubs in the guest rooms,

and a velvet-draped bar. *335 Bowery at 3rd St, T: 212 505 9100, www.theboweryhotel.com*

Hudson Hotel $$$ ❷ 2J/❹

This is legendary hotelier Ian Schrager's fourth NY 'lifestyle hotel'. With sky terrace and two bars. Chic and affordable. *356 W 58th St btw Eighth & Ninth Aves, T: 212 554 6000, www.hudsonhotel.com*

Mercer $$$ ❶ 4D

Red-brick former warehouse with 75 sun-drenched loft-style rooms, minimally furnished. *147 Mercer St at Prince St, T: 212 966 6060, www.mercerhotel.com*

SoHo Grand $$$ ● 3D

Chic 17-story hotel with an industrial-designer lobby and elegant cocktail bar. *310 W Broadway nr Broome St, T: 212 965 3000, www.sohogrand.com*

Boutique Hotels Crosby Street Hotel $$$$ ● 3D

Elegant and whimsical, this British outpost acts as a bright bauble of light on the narrow Crosby Street. It has a bar with terrace and the added luxury of a film club screening room. *79 Crosby St, btw Prince & Spring Sts, T: 212 226 6400, www.firmdalehotels.com*

The Greenwich $$$ ● 3C

In the heart of TriBeCa, this small hotel has the hand-hewn artisanal elegance of a country manor. Spa, pool and gym. *377 Greenwich St btw N Moore & Franklin Sts, T: 212 941 8900, www.thegreenwichhotel.com*

Hotel on Rivington $$ ● 5D

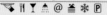

The large minimalist rooms all have floor-to-ceiling windows. *107 Rivington St, T: 212 475 2600, www.hotelonrivington.com*

Library Hotel $$$ ● 3H/❹

Once a library, this 1900 landmark now has the feel of a private club. *299 Madison Ave at 41st St, T: 212 983 4500, www.libraryhotel.com*

The Lowell $$$ ❷ 4J

One of Manhattan's grandest townhouse hotels: discreet but luxurious. *28 E 63rd St btw Madison & Park Aves, T: 212 838 1400, www.lowellhotel.com*

Shoreham Hotel $$$ ❷ 3J/❹

Rooms are smart and stylish and well laid out in a European style. *33 W 55th S, T: 212 247 6700, www.shorehamhotel.com*

Value Hotels

Casablanca Hotel $–$$ ● 3H/❹

Well-managed and comfortable hotel in the heart of Times Square. *147 W 43rd St, T: 212 869 1212, www.casablancahotel.com*

New Yorker Hotel $$ ❷ 2H/❹

This classic art deco hotel offers terrific value along with a collection of spacious and attractive rooms and suites. *481 Eighth Ave at 34th St, T: 212 971 0101, www.newyorkerhotel.com*

The Pod Hotel $$ ❷ 4I

Quiet 'pod' rooms, most with bathrooms. Pod rooms resemble a bright ship's quarters with solo, double and bunk beds. The rooftop garden is a nice area to relax with great views over the city. *230 E 51st St btw Second & Third Aves, T: 212 355 0300, www.thepodhotel.com*

Budget Hotels

Gershwin $ ❶ 3G

One of the best budget hotels in New York. Quirky artwork throughout gives the hotel an interesting edge. Close to the Empire State Building and other midtown attractions. *7 E 27th St nr Third Ave, T: 212 545 8000, www.gershwinhotel.com*

Hotel 91 $ ❶ 5C

This 70-room budget hotel, nestled in the heart of the Lower East Side, is a great location to explore Chinatown, Little Italy and SoHo. Rooms are compact but clean and well equipped. *91 E Broadway, T: 212 266 6800, www.hotel91.com*

Marrakech Hotel $ ❷ 1N

Moroccan-themed rooms with crisp linens and authentic furniture. *2688 Broadway, T: 212 222 2954, www.marrakechhotelnyc.com*

Reservation Agencies
Agencies can offer savings on hotel rack (normal) rates, though often the hotels' own websites will match the offers, without the risk of cancellation fees. Quikbook (*T: 800 789 9887, www.quikbook.com*) and Priceline (*T: 800 774 2354, www.priceline.com*) are popular choices. Priceline's 'Name Your Own Price' option can result in rooms at half price.

Wolcott $ ❶ 3G

Dependable value in a safe, lively part of the Garment District. *4 W 31st St btw Fifth Ave & Broadway, T: 212 268 2900, www.wolcott.com*

Annual Events

January
Winter Antiques Show, *Park Ave & 67th St.*

Chinese New Year: parades through Chinatown.

Restaurant Week (January-February) Great deals at some of New York's finest restaurants. *www.nycgo.com/restaurantweek*

February
Black History Month (all month).

Empire State Building Run-Up: runners ascend 86 floors in 12 mins. *www.nyrr.org/races-and-events*

New York Fashion Week *http://newyorkfashionweek.com*

Westminster Kennel Club Annual Dog Show. *www.westminsterkennelclub.org*

March
St Patrick's Day Parade up Fifth Ave (17 March).

April
New York International Auto Show (mid April). *www.autoshowny.com*

New York Antiquarian Book Fair (mid April). *Park Ave & 67th Sts.* *http://nyantiquarianbookfair.com*

May

Fleet Week: events based around the US Navy and Marine Corps.

Great Five Boro Bike Tour (1st Sunday in May)

Ninth Ave International Food Festival (mid May): mile-long food-fest. *Ninth Ave btw 34th & 57th Sts.* *http://ninthavenuefoodfestival.com*

Memorial Day (last Monday). Beaches open; unofficial first day of summer.

June

National Puerto Rican Day Parade (second Sunday).

Museum Mile Festival: free adm (second Tuesday). *http://museummilefestival.org*

Liberty Challenge (third weekend): Canoe race. Starts at Brooklyn Bridge Park.

Lesbian and Gay Pride Week and March. *www.nycpride.org*

June-August

Central Park SummerStage (*see box, p.35*): free concerts in the park (mid June to mid August). *www.cityparks foundation.org/summerstage*

HBO Bryant Park Summer Film Festival: classic films, jazz and dance. *www.bryantpark.org*

June-September

New York Shakespeare Festival: free Shakespeare in Central Park (*see box, p.31*), T: 212-260-2400, *www.shakespeareinthepark.org*

July

Independence Day (4 July): firework displays all over the city.

Washington Square Music Festival: free concerts in Washington Square Park. *www.washingtonsquare musicfestival.org*

Metropolitan Opera Parks Concerts: free concerts in the park (all month).

Restaurant Week: Great deals at some of New York's finest restaurants. *www.nycgo.com/restaurantweek*

August

Harlem Week Harlem celebrates with a week of parades, art, food and sports events. *http://harlemweek.com*

US Open Tennis Tournament (late August-September). *www.usopen.org*

September

Feast of San Gennaro (third week): 10-day festival of life, food and wine in Little Italy, honoring the patron saint of Naples. *www.sangennaro.org*

New York Film Festival (late September-early October): international art film showcase, Lincoln Center (*see p.31*), *www.filmlinc.com*

Broadway on Broadway: free outdoor concert that kicks off the Broadway season. *www.broadway league.com/broadway-on-broadway*

DUMBO Art Festival (mid September): celebrating art, fashion and music. *http://dumboartsfestival.com/*

October

Columbus Day (second Monday): vast parade up Fifth Avenue.

Halloween Parade (31 October): scary jaunt through Greenwich Village.

Pulaski Parade: Polish heritage celebration. *www.pulaskiparade.com*

November

New York City Marathon (first Sunday): starts on Staten Island, ends in Central Park.

Macy's Thanksgiving Parade (see p.23) down Broadway (fourth Thursday).

The Nutcracker (see p.33) opens at Lincoln Center and the Christmas Spectacular opens at Radio City (Thanksgiving-early January).

December

Illumination of the Christmas tree in Rockefeller Center: The traditional lighting of a huge Christmas tree (first week).

Messiah Sing-In at Lincoln Center: 3,000 participants (mid December).

New Year's Eve: watch the giant ball drop from Times Tower above Times Square (31 January).

Listings

Time Out New York: comprehensive weekly city entertainment listings. *www.timeout.com/newyork*

New York magazine: Weekly magazine, great for its reviews and listings. *http://nymag.com*

Zagat: New York City Restaurants: reliable New York City restaurant guide and listings. *www.zagat.com*

Newspapers

Daily News: Tabloid with a concentration on local news. *www.nydailynews.com*

New York Times: comprehensive news coverage with useful reviews and entertainment listings. *www.nytimes.com*

Wall Street Journal: The world's foremost business newspaper. *http://online.wsj.com*

Further Reading

The Bonfire of the Vanities, **Tom Wolfe**. Morality tale of New York greed and excess.

Under the City Streets, **Pamela Jones**. Sewers to subways.

Delirious New York, **Rem Koolhaas**. Anarchic architecture.

Downtown – My Manhattan, **Pete Hamill**. NYC through the eyes of a veteran reporter.

How the Other Half Lives, **Jacob Riis**. Photography taken of poverty in Lower East Side in 19th century.

Breakfast at Tiffany's, **Truman Capote**. Tale of two people living in 1940s New York. A successful film.

Websites

www.earthcam.com/usa/newyork/timessquare Times Square live from Broadway & 45th St.

www.hopstop.com NYC transit directions, maps, and schedules.

http://mommypoppins.com Things to do in the city with kids.

www.nycgo.com Official tourist board website with everything you want to know about a NYC visit.

http://nymag.com/visitorsguide/ NY Magazine listings

speak it

New Yorkers speak more quickly than other people, sometimes interrupting (in a friendly way) or slurring consonants ('gonna' instead of 'going to').

Though you may occasionally hear the so-called Brooklyn accent ('toidy-toid street'), it is for the most part a faded stereotype dating back to gangs such as the Plug-Uglies and the Bowery B'hoys.

New York argot has been influenced by many different immigrant cultures, including Jewish in the 19th century and Afro-American in the 20th. You'll even hear some surviving 17th-century Dutch words such as 'boss', 'coleslaw', 'cookie' and 'stoop'.

Here are some common examples of NYC speak to help you through your time in the city:

Alphabet City – Avenues A-D in the East Village
Bialy – onion roll
The Big Apple – adopted as NY's official nickname in 1971, first used in the 1920s to refer to the city's famous racetracks or a top-notch booking on Broadway; also a jitterbug dance of the late 1930s
Bodega – Latino corner grocery
Bridge and tunnels – commuters
Bronx cheer – flatulating noise made with tongue, cheeks and lips
Brownstone – 19th-century low house
Chutzpah – cheek
Crosstown bus – east-west bus
Hizzoner – the Mayor
Homies – buddies

Icebox – refrigerator
Korean market – Korean corner shop, with fresh flowers and/ or fruit
Knish (pronounce the k) – dough filled with meat or veg
Ladies' Mile – stretch of Sixth Avenue between 14th & 23rd Streets filled with turn of the century department stores
Lines – queues
Lox – a type of smoked salmon
Mac and cheese – macaroni cheese
Nosh – eat
Schmear – smear of cream cheese on a bagel
Smokes – cigarettes
Stoop – stairs leading up to an apartment building
What gives? – What's going on?
Whazzup? – Hello
Yo – Hello

Whilst every care has been taken to check the accuracy of the information in this guide, the publishers cannot accept responsibility for errors or omissions or the consequences thereof. No part of this guide may be reproduced without the permission of the publishers. Published by Compass Maps Ltd. www.popoutproducts.co.uk © 2014 Compass Maps Ltd.

Written by Vanessa Letts, Kate Poulsson, Fiona Quinn. Updated by Alexis Lipsitz Flippin. Edited by Jenny Haddington. Layout by Angus Dawson. Picture research by Kassia Gawronski.

All pictures: © Compass Maps Ltd and Susannah Sayler except Blue Note p.33. The following courtesy of Dreamstime: Leo Bruce

Hempell (B); Brett Critchley (E); Robert Crum p.1; Gynane p.5L; Maglara p.5R; Cmoulton p.9; Yevgenia Gorbulsky p.12; Sean Pavone p.13L; Mircea Nicolescu p.15; Art2002 p.19; Bo Li p.23; Shiningcolors p.26; Chhobi p.29; Dibrova p.35; Ulrich Mueller p.37L; Julie Feinstein p.40; Manuel3d p.49; Ifeelstock p.52. The following courtesy of Shutterstock: Stuart Monk (A), p.4, p.6; Vitezslav Valka (F); S.Borisov p.1; hansjnh p.1; Andrey Bayda p.3; Erika Cross p.3; ChameleonsEye p.7; Pablo Hidalgo p.8; Asier Villafranca p.10; Erika Cross p.11; Marcio Jose Bastos Silva p.13R; James Steidl p.14; Joshua Haviv p.16; Vacclav p.21L; Marco Rubino p.21R; littleny p.39, p.52; pio3 p.37R, p.54; Gregory James Van Raalte p.45; Judy Kennamer p.47R; Natalia Bratslavsky p.50; Thomas Bedenk p.51; Danger Jacobs p.53; Suranga Weeratunga p.55.

Cover Images: Sandra Baker/ Alamy and Gerald Holubowicz/ Alamy.

This PopOut product, its associated machinery and format use, whether singular or integrated within other products, is subject to worldwide patents granted & pending, including EP1417665, CN ZL02819864.6 & CN ZL200620006638.7. All rights reserved including design, copyright, trademark and associated intellectual property rights. PopOut is a registered trademark and is produced under license by Compass Maps Ltd.
9686

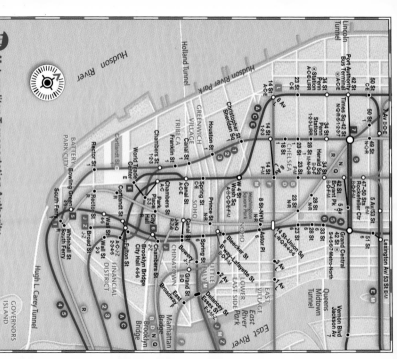